D0710539

AUG 0 8

Regions of the United States: The West

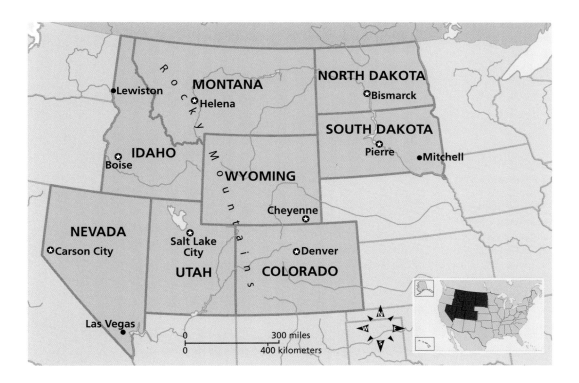

Sally Senzell Isaacs

Chicago, Illinois

Customer Service 888-363-4266

Visit our website at www.heinemannraintree.com

Produced for Raintree by
White-Thomson Publishing Ltd,
Bridgewater Business Centre,
210 High Street, Lewes, BN7 2NH

For information, address the publisher:
Raintree, 100 N. LaSalle, Suite 1200, Chicago, IL 60602

Edited by Susan Crean
Page layout by Clare Nicholas
Photo research by Stephen White-Thomson
Illustrations by John Fleck

11 10 09 08 07
10 9 8 7 6 5 4 3 2 1

**Library of Congress
Cataloging-in-Publication Data**
Isaacs, Sally Senzell, 1950-
  The West / Sally Senzell Isaacs.
     p. cm. -- (Regions of the USA)
  Includes bibliographical references and index.
  ISBN 1-4109-2312-6 (hc) -- ISBN 1-4109-2320-7 (pb)
  1. West (U.S.)--Juvenile literature. I. Title. II. Series.
F591.I73 2007
978--dc22
                    2006004683

Acknowledgments
The publisher would like to thank the following for permission to reproduce photographs:
pp. 4, 10, 13, 14, 15, 26-27, 27B, 31, 35, 40, 41, 44, 48 Viesti Associates; pp. 5, 6, 16, 18, 20, 24, 28, 29, 30, 36-37, 46,
47, 51A Kerrick James; p. 8 Christie's Images/Corbis; pp. 9, 12, 17, 22, 25, 34, 37, 38, 39, 43, 44, 50-51 David Frazier;
p. 11 Corbis; pp. 19, 21, 23 Ron Niebrugge; pp. 32, 33, 49 Nativestock.com; p. 42 The Image Works/Topfoto.

Every effort has been made to contact copyright holders of any material reproduced in this book. Any omissions
will be rectified in subsequent printings if notice is given to the publisher.

Cover photo of Utah's Arches National Park reproduced with permission of Kerrick James.

Contents

Some words are shown in bold, **like this**. You can find out what they mean by looking in the glossary.

The West

The Rockies

The Rockies stretch more than 3,000 miles (4,800 kilometers) from New Mexico to Alaska. The highest peak in the Rockies is Mount Elbert in Colorado. It is 14,433 feet (4,399 meters) high. Mount Elbert is the second highest mountain in the lower 48 states. Mount Whitney in California is 61 feet (18.5 meters) higher.

Big and beautiful are two words often used to describe the West. This is a region known for the Rocky Mountains, the largest chain of mountains in North America. The West itself is made up of some of the biggest states in the country. It has great forests, deep **canyons**, and giant farms and **ranches**.

The West is also known for its wide, open spaces. On a clear day, you can see far into the horizon under the deep, blue western sky. At night there are thousands of stars to see.

The Rocky Mountains, or Rockies, form much of the landscape in the West.

▼

Amazing rock formations such as the ones at Utah's Arches National ➤ Park can be found in many places in the West.

Go west

The West is known as pioneer territory. "We're going west," were the words many parents used to tell their children of their plans to find a better life in the 1840s. There was plenty of open land in the West. It was a good place to start a farm, build a house, and try to have a better life. Thousands of settlers headed west in the 1800s.

Today, people are still traveling west. The fastest growing cities in the country are in this region. Many popular vacation spots are here, too.

Find out later...

What is this impressive natural structure?

Which national park is pictured here?

What is this person doing to this sheep?

You are here

If you look at a map of the United States, you can see that the western states are very big compared to states along the Atlantic Ocean. But while western states are big in size, they are small in **population**.

Wyoming is the tenth largest state in the United States, but it has the fewest people of any state. Montana is so large that these ten eastern states could fit inside it: Maine, Vermont, New Hampshire, Massachusetts, Connecticut, Rhode Island, New York, New Jersey, Delaware, and Maryland. There are fewer people in Montana than in Rhode Island, the nation's smallest state.

Each year nearly a half-million people visit Devils Tower in Wyoming. The tower is made of volcanic rock.

President who made parks

Only one national park is named after a person. That is Theodore Roosevelt National Park in North Dakota. Roosevelt traveled to North Dakota eighteen years before he became president. He fell in love with the land and built a ranch there. After Roosevelt became president in 1901, he approved 5 national parks, 16 national monuments, and 51 national wildlife **refuges**.

Fact file

State	Population	Size
Colorado	4,301,261	104,100 sq. mi. (269,619 sq. km)
Idaho	1,293,953	83,574 sq. mi. (216,456 sq. km)
Montana	902,195	147,046 sq. mi. (380,849 sq. km)
Nevada	1,998,257	110,567 sq. mi. (286,368 sq. km)
North Dakota	642,200	70,704 sq. mi. (183,123 sq. km)
South Dakota	754,844	77,116 sq. mi. (199,730 sq. km)
Utah	2,233,169	84,904 sq. mi. (219,901 sq. km)
Wyoming	493,782	97,809 sq. mi. (253,326 sq. km)

The map shows:

ROCKY MOUNTAINS

MONTANA
• Lewiston
✪ Helena

NORTH DAKOTA
✪ Bismarck

SOUTH DAKOTA
✪ Pierre
• Mitchell

IDAHO
✪ Boise

WYOMING
Cheyenne ✪

NEVADA
✪ Carson City

Salt Lake City ✪
UTAH

Denver ✪
COLORADO

Las Vegas •

0   300 miles
0   400 kilometers

N
W   E
S

Big on beauty

The natural beauty in the West is on a grand scale, too. The West has snow-capped mountains, rocky cliffs, rugged valleys, and roaring rivers. Over the years, people have worried that this natural beauty might be destroyed by development.

The U.S. government has created **national parks** to protect these areas. There are fifteen national parks in the West. In all, these parks cover 8,037 square miles (20,817 square kilometers) of land. Millions of visitors travel to the national parks. Visitors can go hiking, camping, fishing, and rafting in the parks.

A new park

Black Canyon of the Gunnison in Colorado is one of the nation's newest national parks. Though it was designated a national monument in 1933, it became a national park in 1999. The Gunnison River carved through the Rockies to create a deep canyon of dark rock. Black Canyon is up to 2,700 feet (823 meters) deep in some places.

People and History

Long ago, millions of Native Americans lived in the West. Tribes such as the Sioux, Cheyenne, and Mandan lived in the Dakotas. The Shoshone lived in Nevada and Wyoming. The Ute lived in Utah and Colorado. The Blackfoot lived in Montana and the Nez Perce lived in Idaho.

In the 1700s France and Spain claimed much of the land where Native Americans in the West lived. In 1803 President Thomas Jefferson signed the Louisiana Purchase Treaty with France. The United States gained the land between the Mississippi River and the Rocky Mountains. The size of the nation doubled.

The Louisiana Purchase

In 1802 President Jefferson sent Robert Livingston to France to try to buy the port at New Orleans. Livingston returned with much more than New Orleans. France's ruler, Napoleon Bonaparte, was tired of trying to set up colonies in America. He wanted money instead. He told Livingston that the United States could have the entire Louisiana Territory for $15 million. Livingston took him up on the deal and successfully made the Louisiana Purchase.

Native Americans living on the Great **Plains** once lived in foldable homes called teepees.

Fact file

The Missouri River is the longest river in the United States. It stretches from Montana to Missouri, a distance of 2,540 miles (4,090 kilometers).

Explorers of the West

In 1804 President Jefferson chose Meriwether Lewis and William Clark to **explore** the new land. Lewis and Clark set out from a place near St. Louis, Missouri, with three boats and a crew of about 35 people.

Lewis and Clark spent two years, four months, and ten days paddling up the Missouri River, walking through the Rocky Mountains, and bouncing through the **rapids** of the Snake and Columbia Rivers. When they returned, they brought President Jefferson maps and stories about the beautiful land in the West.

Meeting Sacagawea

When Lewis and Clark arrived in North Dakota, a Shoshone woman joined their crew. Her name was Sacagawea. She helped the explorers talk to the Native Americans along the way. With her help the Mandan people drew maps for the explorers. The Shoshone gave them horses.

Sacagawea carried her son, Pomp, for much of the Lewis and Clark ◄ Expedition. This statue in Boise, Idaho, honors them.

9

State names

Spanish and Native American words were used to give many of the states in the West their names. For example, Colorado's state name means "color red" in Spanish, which were the words used to describe the Colorado River. Montana is based on the Spanish word for "mountainous" and Nevada is based on the Spanish word for "snowy." Dakota is the Sioux name for "friend," Utah is named for the Ute Native Americans, meaning "people of the mountains," and Wyoming is based on an Algonquin or Delaware Indian word meaning "large prairie place."

Moving in

Year after year, settlers moved westward. Some went to **mine** for gold and silver in Colorado, Nevada, and Utah. Others went to raise sheep and cattle in Wyoming and Montana or to grow crops in the rich soil of the Dakotas and Idaho.

Settlers built homes, farms, ranches, and towns. The need for better transportation grew. Western farmers and ranchers needed to get their crops and cattle to cities in the east. Factories in the eastern United States wanted to send furniture, clothing, and other things to the West. Little by little, people built railroad tracks to connect western towns to cities in the East.

Some pioneers traveling to Utah pulled their belongings in carts.

Forced out

As settlers moved in, Native Americans were pushed out. The government of the United States sent the U.S. Army to fight against the Native Americans. They were forced to leave their land. Many other Native Americans died from new illnesses that the settlers brought with them.

The government set aside land known as **reservations** for the Native Americans. But this land usually had few trees and poor soil. It was nearly impossible to survive. Before Christopher Columbus arrived from Europe in 1492 there were millions of Native Americans. By 1890 there were less than 250,000.

In 1890 U.S. soldiers attacked about 350 Native Americans near Wounded Knee Creek in South Dakota. These people were among the survivors.

Free land!

Hundreds of thousands of people moved west after President Abraham Lincoln signed the **Homestead Act** in 1862. The government gave 160 acres of free land to people who promised to build a home, grow crops, and live there for five years. These people only needed to fill out the paperwork and pay an $18 fee.

People in the West today

Some of today's westerners are **descendants** of Native Americans. In South Dakota, North Dakota, and Montana, about five to eight people in one hundred are Native American. In the other states, there are fewer Native Americans.

Most people living in the West today are descendants of people from Germany, England, Ireland, and other parts of Europe.

People of Spanish descent live in the West, especially in Colorado and Nevada. In these two states, about one of every five people have families who came from Spanish-speaking countries. In most of the states, only about one or two people in one hundred are African American or Asian.

A new holiday

The people of South Dakota wanted a holiday to celebrate the Native Americans of their past and present. In 1990 South Dakota officially replaced Columbus Day with Native American Day. The day is celebrated on the second Monday each October.

These dancers celebrate the traditions of the Basque region in northern Spain at a festival in Sun Valley, Idaho.

Growing fast

People are still moving west. Recently, Nevada has been the fastest-growing state in the country. More than 200,000 people moved to Nevada between the years 2000 and 2004. Idaho and Utah are also among the fastest growing states.

People move west because land is not as expensive as in other parts of the country. The land is good for farms and ranches. There are also job opportunities in food processing, computer **manufacturing**, and other areas. But most of all, people seem to like the quiet beauty of the West.

Salt Lake City grew from a tiny pioneer town into a city. More than 181,700 people live there today.

City by the lake

The Mormons are a religious group that lived in the eastern United States in the early 1800s. Their neighbors criticized Mormon beliefs, so the Mormons kept moving westward as they looked for a place where they could live. Their leader, Brigham Young, led them to the Great Salt Lake in Utah. Their new community grew into Salt Lake City.

Land in the Area

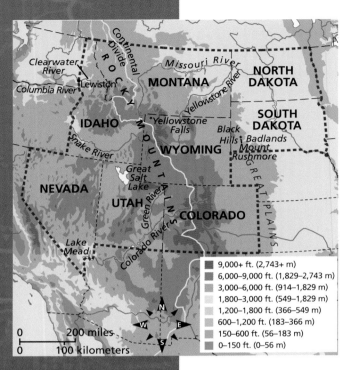

The landforms in the West are many and varied. There are plains, hills, valleys, mountains, canyons, **deserts, mesas**, and more. The Great Plains, which covers roughly one-third of the United States, stretch into Colorado, Wyoming, Montana, North Dakota, and South Dakota. The Rocky Mountains rise into Colorado, Wyoming, Montana, Utah, and Idaho.

The Dakotas

The eastern parts of North Dakota and South Dakota have flat, low **prairies**. The soil is rich, and rain is usually plentiful. There are many farms in this area.

Badlands

Parts of North and South Dakota have deep canyons and steep, flat-topped hills, called mesas. They have been worn away by wind, rain, and snow. French fur trappers referred to this rugged area as "bad lands to cross" in French. It has been known as Badlands ever since.

Badlands National Park may look bare from a distance, but visitors might actually spot a **bison**, deer, or a prairie dog.

The Black Hills

The Black Hills are located in southwestern South Dakota. Unlike the rest of South Dakota, the Black Hills are covered with dense, green pine trees. The Lakota Sioux called the hills *paha sapa*, meaning "hills of black." The Black Hills are sacred for the Sioux and Cheyenne people.

Broken promises

In the Fort Laramie **Treaty** of 1868, the U.S. government promised Native Americans they could keep the Black Hills forever. Then gold was discovered there. Miners rushed in and started digging up the land. Today, the Sioux are fighting in courts to protect the Black Hills. They don't want trees cut down and new roads built. They want their sacred land to be left alone.

► The faces of four U.S. presidents are carved into Mount Rushmore in the Black Hills of South Dakota. They are George Washington, Thomas Jefferson, Theodore Roosevelt, and Abraham Lincoln.

15

Montana

The eastern part of Montana has wide-open plains. But the state got its name from the western part. Montana comes from a Spanish word that means "mountain." The Rocky Mountains run through the western part of the state.

Glacier National Park is in western Montana. Glaciers form when winter snowfall is greater than summer melting. There are more than 50 glaciers in the park. The largest glacier is the Grinnell Glacier. It is 1.5 miles (2.4 kilometers) long and 1 mile (1.6 kilometers) wide. In some places it is 500 feet (150 meters) thick.

These people are hiking on the Grinnell Glacier in Glacier National Park in Montana. Even though it looks like a warm day, the glacier is still frozen solid.

Grasshopper glacier

A scientist found millions of grasshoppers frozen in one of Montana's glaciers. Scientists think the swarm passed over the high mountain and got caught in a snowstorm hundreds or thousands of years ago. People can hike to Grasshopper Glacier. Some hikers have even seen the grasshoppers, although the sight of them is not common.

Idaho

The Rocky Mountains cover nearly half the state of Idaho. It has about 180 peaks that are 10,000 feet (3,048 meters) or higher. Idaho has plenty of water, too. There are more than 2,000 natural lakes and 3,000 miles (4,828 kilometers) of rivers. The Snake River runs through Idaho. Snake River has carved Hell's Canyon, North America's deepest **gorge**.

Idaho has hundreds of waterfalls. Shoshone Falls on the Snake River plunges 212 feet (65 meters). That's more than 40 feet (12 meters) higher than Niagara Falls.

Hell's Canyon has a total length of 125 miles (201 kilometers). About 40 miles (64 kilometers) of it is more than a mile (1.6 kilometers) deep.

Pikes Peak

Pikes Peak in Colorado is probably the most famous mountain in the Rockies, even though it is not the highest. It is popular because there are many ways to climb the peak. Visitors can walk on hiking trails, drive on roads, or take a train. Every year there are running, biking, and even car-racing contests up Pike's Peak. One of the country's most patriotic songs, "America the Beautiful," was written by Katharine Lee Bates in 1893 after she stood on Pikes Peak.

A big boundary

The **Continental Divide** runs along the highest ridges of the Rocky Mountains. It starts in Alaska and goes all the way into Mexico and Central America. It forms part of the boundary between Montana and Idaho and winds through Wyoming and Colorado. The rivers east of the Continental Divide flow to the Atlantic Ocean. Rivers west of the divide flow into the Pacific Ocean.

Colorado and Wyoming

Wyoming and Colorado are known for their tall, beautiful mountains and flat-topped mesas. Both states also have flat land where people have built ranches to raise cattle.

Hundreds of years ago, Native Americans built their homes along canyon walls for protection from enemies. Now these canyons are part of Mesa Verde National Park in Colorado.

Yellowstone National Park

The oldest national park is Yellowstone. It is located in Wyoming and parts of Montana and Idaho. It was named Yellowstone because over millions of years, a volcano spread lava across the land. When the lava cooled, some of it turned into solid, yellow rock.

Today, there is still hot, liquid rock under the ground. It heats underground springs called **geysers**. Sometimes the temperature and pressure of the water cause hot water and steam to shoot out of the ground. Old Faithful is Yellowstone's most famous geyser. It usually erupts every 40 to 70 minutes.

Yellowstone National Park has close to 300 steaming, bubbling geysers. Six of them erupt 100 feet or higher every day.

▼

Super volcano

Scientists tell us that Yellowstone National Park is built on top of an ancient volcano. The volcano erupted 2.1 million years ago, then again 1.3 million years ago, and again 650,000 years ago. The last eruption produced a crater about 47 miles (76 kilometers) long and 28 miles (45 kilometers) wide. Yellowstone Lake is in part of this great crater.

Utah

Millions of years ago, glaciers, volcanoes, and earthquakes cracked and pushed the earth to create canyons throughout southeastern Utah. Wind and rain carved the red rock into arches and bridges.

Long ago there was a huge lake in Utah, which scientists call Lake Bonneville. Over time the water dried up, leaving a dried salt surface that is called the Bonneville Salt Flats. The Flats are 14 miles (22.5 kilometers) long and seven miles (11.2 kilometers) wide. This smooth, flat surface is ideal for racecar and motorcycle driving. Many speed records have been set here.

The Salt Lake

Utah's Great Salt Lake is the largest saltwater lake in the Western Hemisphere. The lake is typically three to five times saltier than the ocean. It is the largest lake between the Mississippi river and the Pacific Ocean.

Some stone formations in Arches National Park in Utah are known as the Windows.

▼

Nevada

The Sierra Nevada mountain range is on the Nevada-California border. Lake Tahoe is located here. It is a popular place for swimming in the summer and skiing in the winter. Nevada has many other mountain ranges. There is gold, silver, copper, and other valuable materials in the mountains.

The mighty Colorado River

The Colorado River forms the Arizona-Nevada border. In 1936 the Hoover Dam was built in Nevada to keep the Colorado River from flooding. It is one of the highest concrete dams in the world. The dam provides water and electric power to cities in the area. Lake Mead was created when the dam was built. It is the largest human-made lake in the United States.

Wall art

There are very old pictures carved in some of the rocks in the Valley of Fire State Park in Nevada. Thousands of years ago, Native Americans carved pictures of animals, people, and other objects. These pictures give us some clues to how the people lived then.

There is enough concrete in the Hoover Dam to make a two-lane highway from San Francisco, California, to New York City.

Forest fires

Dry, hot weather causes dangerous forest fires. Lightning can spark a fire and winds can spread fires. Nevada, Idaho, Colorado, Wyoming, and Montana have suffered from recent forest fires. Firefighters use planes and helicopters to try to put out forest fires.

It is often impossible to reach a forest fire by truck. Planes were used to help put out this fire in Idaho.

➤

Extreme weather

Winters in the West can bring major **blizzards,** with snow piling several feet or meters high. Summers can bring extreme heat and **droughts**. A drought is a long period of time when there is no rain. Nevada is often called the driest state in the country. North Dakota is often called the windiest.

Fact file

In 1936 North Dakota had its highest temperature ever: 121 °F (49 °C). In the same year, it recorded its lowest temperature ever: -60 °F (-51 °C).

Snow

Some areas in the Rockies get as much as 30 feet (9.1 meters) of snow per year. Skiers especially love the powdery snow in Nevada and Utah. The desert air dries out some of the water in the snow clouds before the snow falls. This makes the snow unusually dry.

Weather forecasters watch the wind and snow conditions and try to warn people about **avalanches**. An avalanche is a mass of snow that slides down a mountain. Heavy winds, earthquakes, and even skiers can cause an avalanche. Some avalanches move faster than 100 miles (160 kilometers) an hour. They can bury anyone in their paths.

Fast winds

"Chinook" is the name for strong, warm winds that blow through the Rocky Mountains. They can gust up to 100 miles (161 kilometers) per hour. Sometimes a Chinook can make the temperature rise 50 °F (10 °C) in less than an hour.

Powdery snow falls on Red Canyon in Dixie National Forest in Utah.

Animals and Plants

Dinosaur bones

About 150 million years ago, dinosaurs roamed through northwestern Colorado and northeastern Utah. From 1909 to 1923, about 350 tons of dinosaur bones were removed from this area. Dinosaur National Monument is one of many places in the West to look at dinosaur bones and learn about these animals.

Animals must be strong to survive in the Rocky Mountains. Bighorn sheep, mountain lions, moose, and deer are just a few of the animals that live there. During the summer they find food and shelter in high parts of the mountains. In the winter they move to lower levels where the temperature is warmer. Some grizzly and black bears live in the mountains.

The plains are home to coyotes, deer, and a kind of antelope called the pronghorn. Prairie dogs also live on the plains.

Bighorn sheep can easily scramble up and down narrow ledges of mountain slopes in Montana.
➤

Bison

Before settlers moved to the West there were millions of bison, or buffalo, in the Great Plains. Without the bison, Native Americans could not have survived. They ate bison meat and made bison skins into clothing and tents. As settlers cleared land for building towns and railroads, most of the bison were killed or scared away.

Settlers built homes and roads where the animals once roamed. By 1889 only about 835 bison were left in the United States. Today, bison herds are protected in national parks. Now there may be as many as 200,000 bison.

A herd of buffalo causes a traffic jam in Yellowstone National Park in Wyoming.

Animal talk

Prairie dogs are members of the squirrel family. They dig their homes under the ground and are herbivores, which means they eat plants. For this reason, some people regard prairie dogs as damaging pests. However, prairie dogs may be smarter than some people think. In fact, prairie dogs communicate with each other by using a complex language.

Mountain plants

The mountain areas of the West are covered with pine, spruce, and other evergreen trees. Forests cover 40 percent of Idaho's land area and 30 percent of Utah's.

As you climb higher up the mountains, the plant life changes. Once you reach the **timberline** at about 11,500 feet (3,500 meters), trees cannot grow because it is too cold. Some plants can grow above the timberline. These are low, flowering plants that grow during the short summer months.

Springtime wildflowers bloom in the San Juan Mountains of Colorado.

Desert plants

Few plants can grow in the very dry areas of Utah and Nevada. The cactus plant has a thick stem that can hold water for a long time. Low plants, such as bitter brush, rabbit brush, and sagebrush, also grow in the deserts.

Ancient trees

The bristlecone pine tree is the oldest tree on the earth. Bristlecones are found at Utah's Bryce Canyon National Park and Nevada's Great Basin National Park. The oldest tree in Bryce Canyon is over 1,600 years old. There is an even older bristlecone pine tree in California. It is over 4,765 years old.

Desert plants live in the scorching-hot Valley of Fire State Park in Nevada.

Old plants on display

When Lewis and Clark explored the West, they found 178 plants that were unknown to people east of the Mississippi River. The explorers brought back samples of these plants. Today, you can see these dried and pressed plants in a climate-controlled room at the Academy of Natural Sciences in Philadelphia.

Cities and Towns

Making change

Denver has one of the four United States mints. A mint is a place that makes coins. A tiny D on your coin tells you it was made in Denver. The mint makes between 14 and 20 billion coins a year.

Denver, the capital of Colorado, has the largest population of all the cities in the western region. It is called The Mile-High City. The 15th step of the west side of the state capitol is 5,280 feet (1,609 meters) above sea level. That is exactly one mile!

Denver started as a **trading post** for Arapaho Indians and fur traders. From 1858 through the 1890s, gold and silver were mined in the nearby mountains. The town grew up with stores, banks, restaurants, and hotels for the miners. Farms, ranches, military bases, oil companies, and **tourism** have helped the city grow since then.

People who live and work in Denver can easily drive to the mountains to hike and ski.

Las Vegas, Nevada

Las Vegas and the area around it have the fastest growing population in the country. More than a million and a half people live in the area in and around Las Vegas. One reason people move to Las Vegas is because the land costs less than in many other cities.

Las Vegas is famous for its fancy hotels and **casinos**. There is a volcano and a 20,000-gallon (88,000-liter) aquarium at the Mirage. The Venetian provides boat rides on a canal, just like in Venice, Italy. The Luxor is shaped like an Egyptian pyramid, and guests ride an "inclinator," which is an elevator that moves at an angle.

Bright lights from big hotels light up the Las Vegas sky.

▼

A grand hotel

The MGM Grand Hotel Casino is the second largest hotel in the world and the largest hotel in North America. The hotel has 5,034 guest rooms. A 45-foot (13.7 meter) tall bronze lion statue sits at the hotel's front entrance. It is the largest bronze statue in the United States. Hotel guests can also visit real lions in the hotel's Lion Habitat.

Salt Lake City, Utah

Salt Lake City has the third-largest **metropolitan area** in the region. It is Utah's largest city and capital. Mormons founded it in 1847. When the city started, the streets were laid out in a grid-like pattern around the Mormon Temple. It took 40 years to build the temple. Mountains surround Salt Lake City. It was the site of the 2002 Winter Olympics.

Boise, Idaho

Boise is Idaho's largest city and capital. Like Denver, Boise started as a mining town after an 1862 gold rush. Later, it grew because of lumber, farming, and hi-tech businesses.

Bring up the heat!

The capitol building in Boise is heated by pumping natural hot water from 3,000 feet (914 meters) below the ground. Hot volcanic rock heats the underground water. This is called **geothermal** heat. Many other buildings in Boise also use geothermal heat. Using geothermal heat reduces air pollution. Compared to other heating systems, the cost to use geothermal heat is very low.

More than 2,500 athletes from about 80 countries came to Salt Lake City for the 2002 Winter Olympics.
▼

Small towns

In 1864 gold was discovered in Last Chance Gulch, Montana. Miners rushed in, put up their tents, and tried to get rich. After the gold rush, some people stayed and helped build the city. Its name was changed to Helena. It is the capital of Montana, with a population of 25,780.

Park City, Utah, has a small population of about 7,300 people. It has become world famous because of the annual Sundance Film Festival. In 1981 the actor Robert Redford started the festival as a place for young filmmakers to share their work. Now, more than 40,000 people come to Park City for the festival.

Old Deseret Village shows what life was like for pioneers in This Is the Place State Park in Utah.

Ghost towns

Some mining towns grew, while others died. Often, when the gold and silver ran out, the miners left town. Stores and offices shut down. The town became a ghost town. There were many ghost towns in the West. Today, some are tourist attractions. In Silver City, Idaho, old buildings are still standing, including houses, a hotel, drug store, barbershop, and school.

Fact file
Of the eight western states, South Dakota has the smallest capital city. Fewer than 20,000 people live in Pierre.

31

Rural Life

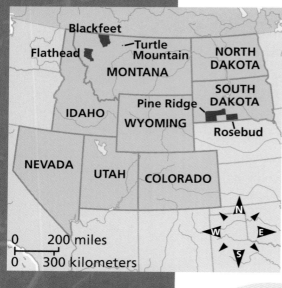

Blackfeet
Flathead
Turtle Mountain
MONTANA
NORTH DAKOTA
SOUTH DAKOTA
Pine Ridge
IDAHO
WYOMING
Rosebud
NEVADA
UTAH
COLORADO

0   200 miles
0   300 kilometers

N
W   E
S

As settlers moved west, they wanted Native Americans to move out of their way. The United States government and Native American groups made treaties. The Native Americans gave up their land in exchange for land on a reservation.

As more settlers moved westward, the government took land away from the reservations. Native Americans are still trying to protect their land. Today, Native Americans live in cities and towns all over the West. But many still live on reservations such as the ones on the map.

Wind River Reservation

The Eastern Shoshone people were not forced to move to Wind River Reservation in Wyoming. It was already their winter hunting grounds. The Shoshone's Chief Wasakie asked the government for the Shoshone reservation to be made on this land. Later, the government moved the Northern Arapaho to the reservation. Both groups still share the Wind River Reservation.

Basketball is one of many sports that people who live on the Pine Ridge Reservation in South Dakota enjoy.

A hard life

The Pine Ridge Reservation in South Dakota is home to more than 14,000 Oglala Lakota Sioux. The reservation is 2.7 million acres (1,092,651 hectares), which is roughly the size of Connecticut. The reservation includes schools, a post office, and homes.

The Badlands and grassy plains are beautiful, and the people have a rich culture of stories, art, and music. But there are many problems on this reservation. It is one of the poorest places in the country. Most people cannot find jobs. Most homes have no running water.

The West's main reservations

Name	State(s)	Native American Population, 2000
Pine Ridge	South Dakota	14,484
Rosebud	South Dakota	9,165
Blackfeet	Montana	8,684
Turtle Mountain	North Dakota	8,043
Flathead	Montana	7,883

Casinos on reservations

Reservations have their own laws and do not have to follow many of their state's laws. This is why gambling is allowed on reservations. Even if a state does not allow gambling, the reservation can allow it. Casinos on reservations provide jobs for Native Americans.

Life on the Pine Ridge Reservation has changed greatly since it was first established in the late 1800s.

Farms and ranches

Cattle for beef is raised on western ranches. One hundred years ago, most people in the West lived and worked on small farms and ranches. But that has changed. Fewer people live and work on farms and ranches than once did. Today, modern machines do most of the work.

On a western ranch, wide-open spaces are still all around you. It's a long drive to school, stores, and neighbor's houses.

Ranch vacations

Some ranches in the West welcome visitors who want to feel what it is like to live on a ranch. Tourists who visit these ranches can take care of animals, ride horses, and cook over a campfire.

Cowhands keep cattle from wandering away from the rest of the herd.

Farming

Everything from onions and potatoes to sunflowers and cherries are grown on millions of acres of land in the West. Much of the nation's wheat, barley, and oats are grown on farms in the West. Family farms are not as common as they once were. As with ranches, much of the work is now done by machines.

The success of crops in the region depends on the amount of rainfall. For example, crops grow well in North Dakota's Red River Valley, while ranches are more common in the southwest of the state and in other states such as Wyoming, where it is drier. Wyoming only gets about 10 inches (25 centimeters) of rainfall each year.

Watch the weather

People on farms and ranches think a lot about the weather. When there is no rain, the crops may die. If the grass dies, the animals could starve. In recent years, the western region has suffered from several dry periods.

▼ These South Dakota farmers are spraying the crops to kill damaging insects.

Getting Around

E.T. Highway

People call Route 375 in Nevada the "Extraterrestrial Highway." This is because people have reported seeing UFOs there. Perhaps the UFOs are really planes taking off from a nearby military base known as Area 51. In the 1950s, Area 51 was used for testing spy planes. Since then, many kinds of aircraft have been tested there. The military keeps the details of these missions top secret.

Cities in the West are not near to one another. It can take more than eight hours to drive across Montana. Interstate 70 in Utah is one of the quietest stretches of highway in the nation. You could drive almost 100 miles without seeing a town or gas station. Since it takes so long to drive between cities, many people fly instead.

Mountain tunnel

The world's highest road tunnel is the Eisenhower-Johnson Memorial Tunnel. It is west of Denver. The tunnel is 11,158 feet (3,401 meters) above sea level. In the winter many mountain roads are closed due to snow and ice.

Many people call the Beartooth Highway one of the most beautiful highways in the nation. Tourists can drive on it from Custer National Forest in Montana to Yellowstone National Park in Wyoming.

Moving products

Highways and railroads connect the West to other parts of the country. Trucks and trains carry lumber, coal, farm products, and factory-made goods to other cities.

Lewiston, Idaho, is called the farthest inland seaport in the West. It is a full state away from the Pacific Ocean. Despite this, boats can travel on the Snake and Columbia Rivers to the ocean. That makes Lewiston a bustling place. Trucks and trains arrive with western farm and forest products. The products are loaded onto boats that go to 40 different countries.

Grain is stored by the Snake River in Lewiston, Idaho, before ships transport it to other countries.

Coast-to-coast tracks

In the 1860s railroad tracks were needed across the nation. The Central Pacific Railroad built tracks from California eastward. The Union Pacific Railroad built tracks from Nebraska westward. On May 10, 1869 the two tracks met at Promontory, Utah. Leland Stanford, one of Central Pacific's leaders, hit the last spike with a silver hammer.

37

Work in the Area

Potato power

Idaho grows more potatoes than any other state. Each year Idaho grows just less than one-third of the potatoes in the United States. More than half of Idaho's potatoes are processed into foods such as potato chips and frozen French fries. Every year, Americans consume about 130 pounds (60 kilograms) of potatoes per person.

There are many kinds of jobs in the West. As in the past, farms, ranches, and mines remain important to the West. For example, farm hands operate the machines that plant the crops in the spring and **harvest** them in the fall. Farm managers decide how to keep the soil healthy, how many crops to plant, and when and where to sell the crops. Offices and factories have become important places of work as well.

In 2005 Idaho grew more than 11.5 billion pounds (5.2 billion kilograms) of potatoes.

Ranch work

Ranchers raise cattle sold for beef. Montana's ranches alone have 2.7 million cattle. Ranch workers, called wranglers, ride horses as they lead herds of cattle to grazing pastures. As the weather changes and the cattle eat grass, the wranglers round up the cattle and move them to other pastures.

Ranchers must be sure that cattle stay healthy. They make sure that food is plentiful, and they call a veterinarian when cattle get sick. Ranchers also **breed** their cattle so that new calves are born every year.

Sheep products

Wyoming, South Dakota, Colorado, Montana, and Utah are among the top states for raising sheep. In 2002 Wyoming had 460,000 sheep. Some sheep are sold for meat. Others are kept on ranches. Their wool is used to make clothing, carpeting, and blankets.

Expert sheep shearers remove the wool from sheep at a ranch in Idaho. Later, the wool will be turned into yarn to make clothing and other products.

Other jobs

Most people in the West work in service jobs. They work in stores, banks, hospitals, and offices. There are also many jobs in manufacturing. These jobs include making food products, computers, and airplanes.

Protecting our country

The U.S. Air Force Academy is located in Colorado Springs, Colorado. Young men and women train to be officers in the U.S. Air Force. NORAD is the North American Aerospace Defense Command. It is located deep inside Cheyenne Mountain, which overlooks Colorado Springs. NORAD has equipment that can watch for and warn the public of attacking aircraft, missiles, or space vehicles.

Lumber

Many products are made from western forests. Factories turn the wood into paper, boxes, building materials, furniture, pencils, telephone poles, toothpicks, and baseball bats. Lumber companies must practice good forest management. This means they must plant new trees when they cut down grown trees.

More than 36,000 students have graduated from the U.S. Air Force Academy in Colorado Springs.

40

Welcoming visitors

Many people take vacations in the West. They travel there to visit the hotels in Las Vegas, mountain ski **resorts**, national parks, and ranches. Tourism is one of the fastest growing industries in the region.

Many people living in the western region have jobs related to tourism. Some serve other people. There are hotel workers who clean rooms and cook food. Other people work in national parks, teach ski lessons, and guide rafts through the rivers.

Mining

The gold rushes ended years ago, but mining is still important in the western region. There is still gold, silver, copper, and coal in the ground. But as the prices paid for these minerals dropped and the cost of mining increased, many mines closed.

◀ These men dress up like men of the Wild West and entertain tourists in Deadwood, South Dakota.

Free Time

Many people call Las Vegas the "Entertainment Capital of the World." Every night there are dozens of spectacular shows at the hotels. People can watch famous entertainers, glamorous dancers, and all kinds of performers from magicians to ice skaters.

Mountain concerts

Imagine sitting among giant red rocks in the Rocky Mountains. The stars are above you. Your favorite band is on stage. The Red Rocks **Amphitheater** near Morrison, Colorado, is the perfect setting for a concert. They say Mother Nature is the architect of this amphitheater, where the audience sits between two 300-foot (91.4-meter) rocks.

Authors of South Dakota

Two famous authors are from South Dakota: Frank Baum, author of *The Wonderful Wizard of Oz* lived in Aberdeen. Laura Ingalls Wilder, author of *Little House on the Prairie* lived in De Smet.

Costumes, dancing, scenery, and music are all part of Las Vegas-style entertainment!

Cowboy music

Cowboy poetry and music festivals are held throughout the West. Cowboy music goes back to the days when cowhands traveled on the cattle trails. Cowhands sang songs and whistled to entertain themselves and keep the cattle calm.

Art museums

There are many art museums in the West. One is the C.M. Russell Museum in Great Falls, Montana. The museum is named after Charles Russell, who spent much of his life in Montana. He became a cowboy and painted about life on the cattle trails. Native American art and crafts are also on display at museums in the West.

Who can saw a tree trunk the fastest? That's what this contest in Boise, Idaho, is all about.

Yodeling

Some western singers are known for their yodeling. When they yodel, their voices go high and low quickly.

Try singing this: "Hodl-ay–EE-ee." Make your voice higher when you sing EE.

Food

People say that the West is meat and potatoes country. What would you expect from the cattle and potato capitals of the nation? A typical western party might have a "chuck-wagon cookout." The chuck wagon was the cook's wagon on the cattle trail. Today, a chuck-wagon cookout is a barbecue.

Big on game

Westerners cook up lots of other kinds of meat. Restaurant menus list deer meat, rabbit, and rattlesnake. Chislic is a traditional food in South Dakota. It is made of chunks of venison, beef, and lamb on a thin stick.

This man just won the Buffalo Chili Eating Contest in Custer State Park, South Dakota. ➤

Fact File

Kuchen is a sweet German cake topped with peaches, apples, or other fruit. It is the official dessert of South Dakota.

Potatoes!

Idaho is famous for its potatoes. People living in the state have recipes for everything from potato pancakes and potato bread to potato doughnuts. Of course, the French fry is Idaho's favorite way to eat potatoes. Each year 4.5 billion pounds of French fries are sold in the United States. Two-thirds of all the processed potatoes in the United States come from Idaho.

Potato facts

A potato is 80 percent water and 20 percent solid. It takes 10,000 pounds of potatoes to make 3,500 pounds of potato chips. In the United States, a pound of potato chips costs 200 times more than a pound of potatoes!

The West has many factories with machines that wash, sort, and cut potatoes into French fries.

The great outdoors

Winter weather does not stop people in the West from going outdoors. In fact, skiing and snowboarding are among the most popular sports in all eight of the states in the region. There are ski trails for everyone. Beginners start on wide gentle slopes. Expert skiers can race at a speed of 65 miles (105 kilometers) per hour.

Most people ride a chair lift to the top of the mountain. The chairs are attached to a cable that moves upward. A few resorts offer a helicopter ride to the mountaintop. The helicopter takes the skiers away from the main ski trails.

This Colorado skier is trying out some fancy footwork. ◄

Summer fun

There's plenty of fun in the summer months, too. Some outdoor activities include taking a hike in the mountains, fishing in a stream, or paddling a raft through wild river rapids.

Whitewater rafting combines the fun of a roller coaster and the beauty of a mountain hike. Several people paddle a raft down the river. Everyone must listen for the swooshing of the rapids ahead and then steer carefully through them. It's impossible to stay dry as the water splashes over the raft.

Whitewater rafting is popular in Colorado. It is a sport that requires courage, skill, and protective helmets.

Pro teams

Westerners love their sports teams. Denver fans cheer for the Colorado Rockies baseball team, Denver Nuggets basketball team, Denver Broncos football team, and Colorado Avalanche hockey team. Salt Lake City basketball fans follow the Utah Jazz (NBA) and the Utah Starzz (WNBA). All the states have exciting college sports.

Western festivals

Rodeos are held throughout the West. Cowboys and cowgirls compete to see who can stay on a **bucking bronco** the longest and who can catch a calf the fastest. Many high schools have rodeo teams. Rodeos might also have a stock show where ranchers show off prized cattle, horses, goats, and sheep.

Once a year, the tiny town of Reedpoint, Montana, celebrates its sheep. People let hundreds of sheep run for six blocks down Main Street. The event is followed by a parade and contests with prizes.

The friendship garden

Many festivals and events are held in the International Peace Garden. North Dakota and Manitoba, Canada, share the Garden. It is a symbol of friendship between Canada and the United States. Over 150,000 flowers bloom in the garden. There are growing floral displays of the U.S. and Canadian flags.

This young rodeo rider at the Little Britches Rodeo in Pikes Peak, Colorado, is doing a great job staying on the bull.

➤

Follow the dogs

Dogs are the stars of Wyoming's International Pedigree Stage Stop Sled Dog Race. Dogs pull sleds from Jackson Hole, Wyoming, to Park City, Utah. They stop in six different towns along the way. People in the towns celebrate with dog parades, ice sculpture contests, fishing contests, and carnivals.

Powwows

Native Americans hold colorful festivals called powwows. Family and friends come from across the country for these special events. Some powwows have parades, craft fairs, horse races, and rodeos. Drumming contests are very popular, as are Native American dances. Traditional foods are served, including a fruit pudding called wojapi.

The pin palace

The National Bowling Stadium in Reno, Nevada, has been called Pin Palace. There are 78 lanes in a space larger than a football field. There is the world's longest video screen to display scores. A high-tech ball return sends the ball back at speeds in excess of 30 miles (48 kilometers) an hour.

Native American dancing is an ancient tradition that is celebrated at festivals today.

49

An Amazing Region

The West of today combines Native American roots, the spirit of the pioneers and settlers, and the dream of an exciting future.

Westerners are proud of their history and look forward to sharing it with visitors. It is a world of national parks and rural ranches and farms, where the buffalo once roamed and cowboys thrived. It is a world where the wild west was once alive, where miners went to strike it rich, and where pioneering families hoping for a better life settled.

Popular parks

In 2004 Yellowstone National Park (Wyoming, Montana, Idaho) was the sixth most visited national park in the United States. There were 2,868,317 visitors. Zion National Park (Utah) was number eight with 2, 677,342 visitors. Grand Teton National Park (Wyoming) was number nine with 2,360,373. Rocky Mountain National Park is the most visited park in the region.

Tourists seem to be as far from city life as they can get, as they ride by Devils Tower National Monument in Wyoming. ◄

What's next

Modern life has brought new resorts, homes, and factories to the western region. People once found jobs in farming, ranching, and mining. Today, they are turning to work in the service industry, manufacturing, or technology. These people still treasure the spirit of the West.

Despite big changes, wide-open spaces still fill much of the countryside in the West. The mountains and plains are as beautiful as they were 200 years ago. They still attract people who want to leave the big cities behind.

No matter what else happens in the world, Yellowstone's most famous geyser, Old Faithful, stays on schedule. ◄

Famous tower

Devils Tower in Wyoming is a volcano-like tower. It is a sacred site of worship for many Native Americans. Theodore Roosevelt named Devils Tower as the nation's first national monument on September 24, 1906. The hills surrounding the tower are covered with pine forests and prairie grasslands. Deer, prairie dogs, and other wildlife thrive in the area.

Find Out More

World Wide Web

The Fifty States
www.infoplease.com/states.html

This site has a clickable U.S. map that gives facts about each of the 50 states, plus images of each state's flag.

These sites have pictures, statistics, and other facts about each state in the region:

American West
www.Americanwest.com

Colorado
www.colorado.gov

Idaho
www.accessidaho.gov

Montana
www.mt.gov

Nevada
www.nv.gov

North Dakota
www.nd.com

South Dakota
www.state.sd.us

Utah
www.utah.gov

Wyoming
www.wyoming.gov

Books to read

Bruchen, Kelli. *Bristlecone Pines*. San Diego: Kidhaven Press, 2005.

Foulk, Karen. *147 Fun Things to Do in Salt Lake City*. Into Fun Company Publications, 2002.

Isaacs, Sally Senzell. *The American Adventure: The Lewis and Clark Expedition*. Chicago: Heinemann Library, 2004.

Isaacs, Sally Senzell. *The American Adventure: The Oregon Trail*. Chicago: Heinemann Library, 2004.

Marsh, Carole. *The Mystery in the Rocky Mountains*. Peachtree City, GA: Gallopade International, 2004.

Places to visit

Arches National Park (Moab, Utah)
  View more than 2,000 national sandstone arches at this national park.

C.M. Russell Museum (Great Falls, Montana)
  This museum houses a collection of western art.

Craters of the Moon National Monument (Arco, Carey, and Rupert, Idaho)
  Here you can view three young lava fields and other volcanic features.

Devils Tower National Monument (Devils Tower, Wyoming)
  The tower itself in addition to rolling hills are found in this national park.

Red Rocks Amphitheater (Morrison, Colorado)
  This natural amphitheater is in an amazing scenic area.

Yellowstone National Park (Wyoming, Montana, and Idaho)
  This huge national park includes all kinds of geothermal wonders.

Timeline

1500
Native Americans have been living throughout the West for thousands of years.

1540
Spanish explorers reach the western region.

1743
French explorer, Pierre De la Verendrye, discovers the Rocky Mountains while searching for a western sea.

1803
United States buys Louisiana Purchase from France. It includes the Dakotas, Montana, Wyoming, Colorado, and part of Idaho.

1804–1806
Lewis and Clark explore the western region as they go from Missouri to the Pacific Ocean.

1812
Robert Stuart discovers a route through the Rocky Mountains (South Pass), which will become part of the Oregon Trail.

1843
Some 1,000 men, women, and children leave Missouri on the Oregon Trail. They pass through parts of the western region on their way to Oregon and California.

1847
Mormons reach Utah and set up a community by the Great Salt Lake.

1858
Gold is discovered in Colorado, setting off a gold rush there.

1860
Pony Express service begins, taking mail on horseback from St. Joseph, Missouri, to Sacramento, California.

1861
The first transcontinental telegraph lines meet at Salt Lake City, Utah; Pony Express service ends.

1862
The Homestead Act gives free land for building homes in the West.

1869
The first transcontinental railroad is completed at Promontory, Utah.

1872
Yellowstone becomes the nation's first national park.

1873
The invention of barbed wire lets ranchers fence off their cattle and divide up the wide-open spaces.

1876
The Sioux and Cheyenne defeat Lt. Colonel Custer at the Battle of Little Bighorn in Montana.

1886
An icy, stormy winter kills hundreds of thousands of cattle in the West.

1890
All Native Americans now live on reservations; at Wounded Knee, South Dakota, the last battle is fought.

1931
Gambling becomes legal in Nevada, giving Las Vegas its start as the "Entertainment Capital of the World."

1951
Idaho Falls generates the world's first electricity from nuclear energy.

1980
Mount St. Helens erupts, covering northern Idaho with volcanic ash; the volcano had been inactive since 1857.

1988
Forest fires burn one-third of Yellowstone National Park.

1993
Colorado Rockies become the first major league baseball team in the region.

2000
Wild fires destroy over a million acres of western land.

2002
Salt Lake City hosts the Winter Olympics.

States at a Glance

Colorado

Became State: 1876
Nickname: The Centennial State
Motto: *Nil sine Numine*—Nothing without Providence
Capital: Denver
State Bird: Lark bunting
State Tree: Blue spruce
State Flower: Rocky Mountain columbine
State Animal: Rocky Mountain bighorn sheep
State Song: "Where Columbines Grow"

Idaho

Became State: 1890
Nickname: The Gem State
Motto: *Esto Perpetua*—It is forever
Capital: Boise
State Bird: Mountain bluebird
State Tree: Western white pine
State Flower: Syringa
State Animal (Horse): Appaloosa
State Song: "Here We Have Idaho"

Montana

Became State: 1889
Nickname: The Treasure State
Motto: *Oro y plata*—Gold and silver
Capital: Helena
State Bird: Western meadowlark
State Tree: Ponderosa pine
State Flower: Bitterroot
State Animal: Grizzly bear
State Song: "Montana"

Nevada

Became State: 1864
Nickname: The Silver State
Motto: All for Our Country
Capital: Carson City
State Bird: Mountain bluebird
State Tree: Bristlecone pine
State Flower: Sagebrush
State Animal: Desert bighorn sheep
State Song: "Home Means Nevada"

North Dakota

Became State: 1889
Nickname: Peace Garden State
Motto: Liberty and Union, Now and Forever, One and Inseparable
Capital: Bismarck
State Bird: Western meadowlark
State Tree: American elm
State Flower: Wild prairie rose
State Animal (Horse): Nakota breed
State Song: "North Dakota Hymn"

South Dakota

Became State: 1889
Nickname: The Mount Rushmore State
Capital: Pierre
Motto: Under God the People Rule
State Bird: Ring-necked pheasant
State Tree: Black Hills spruce
State Flower: Pasqueflower
State Animal: Coyote
State Song: "Hail, South Dakota"

Utah

Became State: 1896
Nickname: Beehive State
Capital: Salt Lake City
Motto: Industry
State Bird: Gull
State Tree: Blue spruce
State Flower: Sego lily
State Animal: Rocky Mountain elk
State Song: "Utah, We Love Thee"

Wyoming

Became State: 1890
Nickname: Equality State
Capital: Cheyenne
Motto: Equal Rights
State Bird: Western meadowlark
State Tree: Cottonwood
State Flower: Indian paintbrush
State Mammal: Bison (North American buffalo)
State Song: "Wyoming"

Glossary

amphitheater building with seats rising in curved rows around an open space. Plays, concerts, and games are performed in the open space.

avalanche mass of snow that slides down a mountain

bison large animal with shaggy head; also called North American buffalo

blizzard blinding snowstorm with strong winds

breed produce offspring

bucking bronco untamed horse that is not used to having a rider

canyon narrow valley with high, steep sides

casino building or room used for gambling, or playing games of risk for money

Continental Divide line of summits in the Rocky Mountains

descendants people who come from those before them

desert dry land with few plants

drought long period of time when there is no rain

explore look, for the purpose of finding something new

geothermal using the heat of the earth's interior

geyser spring that shoots out steam and hot water

glacier thick, slow-moving sheet of ice

gorge deep, narrow valley, like a canyon

harvest bring in crops after they have grown

Homestead Act law passed in the 1860s whereby settlers could claim 160 acres of land if they built a house, planted crops, and stayed for five years

manufacturing turning something into a useful product

mesa steep hill with flat top

metropolitan area region that includes a city and the suburbs around it

mine 1. dug-out place from which minerals (gold, silver, coal) are taken 2. take minerals out of the earth

national park place set aside to protect the land, plants, and animals

plains wide area of flat or gently rolling land. The Great Plains is land between the Mississippi River and the Rocky Mountains.

population number of people living in a state or region

prairie wide area of flat or gently rolling land

ranch large farm where herds of cattle, sheep, or horses are raised

rapids part of a river where the water runs fast, usually over rocks

refuge place that provides protection or shelter

resort place where vacationers go for fun and relaxation

reservation land set aside by the government for Native Americans to live on

rodeo show that features cowboy skills, such as riding and roping

timberline upper part of a mountain where trees do not grow

tourism business of providing services and entertainment to travelers

trading post a place where people could exchange goods in an area with few towns and people

treaty written agreement

Index